THE LOOK OF THINGS

HENRI COLE

THE LOOK OF THINGS

ALFRED A KNOPF

New York   1995

AUTHOR'S NOTE For their encouragement, I would like to record my thanks to editors of the following publications, where poems, sometimes in different form, were originally published.

ANTAEUS "The Look of Things"
BOULEVARD "The New Life"
COLUMBIA: A MAGAZINE OF POETRY & PROSE "Tarantula" and "Three Aurelian Moons"
THE HARVARD REVIEW "Eating Figs under the White Rocks"
HUBBUB "The Cabbage Butterfly" and "Swimming with the Dead"
THE NATION "Aix"
THE NEW REPUBLIC "The Pink and the Black"
THE NEW YORKER "40 Days and 40 Nights," "Immaculate Mary Breathes the Air We Breathe," "Plastilina," "You Come When I Call You," "Carnations" and "Paper Dolls"
THE OHIO REVIEW "The Housekeeper and the Handyman"
THE ONTARIO REVIEW "Crayola"
THE PARIS REVIEW "Sacrament," "The Christological Year," "Une Lettre à New York," "Marius, Son of Sarkis, Named for the Roman Consul, Savior from the Barbarians, Putative Husband of Mary Magdalene"
PRAIRIE SCHOONER "Palette" and "Katrina's Bedroom"
PROVINCETOWN ARTS "The Roman Baths at Nîmes"
SOUTHWEST REVIEW "The Gondolas"
THE THREEPENNY REVIEW "Ex-voto"
THE VILLAGE VOICE "Irradiation"
WESTERN HUMANITIES REVIEW "Torso"
THE YALE REVIEW "Christmas at Carthage," "The Bird Show at Aubagne," "The Minimum Circus" and "Apostasy"

I would also like to record my thanks to the Trustees of the Amy Lowell Poetry Travelling Scholarship and the Ingram Merrill Foundation, as well as the Literature Program of the National Endowment for the Arts, for financial awards during the composition of this book, and to the Camargo Foundation, the Corporation of Yaddo and the MacDowell Colony for their gracious hospitality during residencies.

Library of Congress Cataloging-in-Publication Data
The look of things: poems/by Henri Cole.—1st ed.
p. cm.
ISBN 0–679–43352–X
I. Title.
PS3553.04725L66 1995
811'.54—dc20   94–23297
                                CIP

Manufactured in the United States of America
First Edition

To Harry Ford

And least will guess that with our bones
We left much more, left what still is
The look of things, left what we felt

At what we saw.

Wallace Stevens
A Postcard from the Volcano

Contents

I

I I

I I I

I

The Pink and the Black

The sea a goblet of black currant liqueur.
The pink sky regarding me sadly.
The hand that was mine, motionless,
   between passages in a story.
The sucking sound of underwater breathing, spitting.
The limy bubbles sequining the sea.
The mutable shape we call man, rising out of it,
   all nostrils and lips behind glass.
The Day-Glo flippers striking against limestone
   like a Spanish fan on pearls.
The limp, sac-like bodies, pink suckers in perfect rows,
   hooked at the belt.
The oyster-white rock on which we sat.
The sleepy face that looked at me.
The crossed ankles.
The inky cloud, like an octopus's secretion,
   moving overhead.
The sun a watery white mess.
The dainty, crocheted net where the sea urchins slept.
The long spines of the one shucked for me.
The bowie knife, sharp as a curate's words, cutting, cutting.
The intractable sea flattening and flattening.
The metallic back of something escaping,
   reveling beneath the shadows.
I had been so lonely, hungry as a snake.

Sacrament

On the way to Mass, by chance,
I spotted you on the boulevard at a café
with your wife and her mother.
You were wearing the lovely gold cross
my father gave me when I was a boy.
After each sip of her drink,
your wife tucked her bangs behind her ears,
recrossed her china white legs.
I have given you back to her,
locked the letters in a box.
Laughing at something being said,
you raised your arm in the same gesture
as the night we met in the park,
when a woman walking a terrier spat at us.
Do you remember the wet, odorless grass
in which we sat, how it shone
like the back of an animal?
At one point your wife's mother
reached across in an impassioned way
and brushed something from your sweater,
as if the fur of that animal
was what she'd seen
and with her hand wanted to say
they wouldn't let you go again.

The Gondolas

It has been so long since he left his country
that he cannot remember its face.
At the arena for athletes nobody sees what he is thinking.
Christopher Columbus, at the stadium gates, points to the New
　　World.
A dozen perfect crystallizations of flesh sprint on the field.
Above them gondolas dangle from a cable
rising to the mountaintop.
It has been so long since the illness that he cannot remember
what drew him from the prairie.
What he hears is not Miguel sailing through the porcelain sky,
hollering for him like the archangel,
but the battered past,
the years of implacable longing so long ago
in parks and darkened rooms where others like him were known
　　to go.
"Let this be clear," a voice in immaculate speech is saying,
"This man loved earth, not heaven, enough to die."
And the Ferris wheel by the sea rolled over and over,
no less than the sea itself
pummeling Columbus's three little ships,
trying and trying to be lifted by it.

The Look of Things

If my family has regrets,
it's over gin and furtive sex;
the General, my brother, tries—
refusing any compromise—
to keep his sons from knowing me.
What sweeter honey to the bee
than denial? Waved away
it zeros back. What shall I say
to those who years from now will come
to rectify the past. If one
of us succumbs to drunkenness,
let it be love that tips the glass.

40 Days and 40 Nights

Opening a vein he called my radial,
the phlebotomist introduced himself as Angel.
Since the counseling it had been ten days
of deep inversion—self-recrimination weighed
against regret, those useless emotions.
Now there would be thirty more enduring the notion
of some self-made doom foretold in the palm.

Waiting for blood work with aristocratic calm,
big expectant mothers from Spanish Harlem
appeared cut-out, as if Matisse had conceived them.
Their bright smocks ruffling like plumage before the fan,
they might themselves have been angels, come by land.

Consent and disclosure signed away, liquid gold
of urine glimmering in a plastic cup, threshold
of last doubt crossed, the red fluid was drawn
in a steady hematic ooze from my arm.
"Now, darling, the body doesn't lie," Angel said.
DNA and enzymes and antigens in his head
true as lines in the face in the mirror
on his desk.

        I smiled, pretending to be cheered.
In the way that some become aware of God
when they cease becoming overawed
with themselves, no less than the artist concealed
behind the surface of whatever object or felt
words he builds, so I in my first week
of waiting let the self be displaced by each
day's simplest events, letting them speak
with emblematic voices that might teach me.
They did . . . until I happened on the card

from the clinic, black-framed as a graveyard.
Could the code 12 22 90 have represented
some near time, December 22, 1990, for repentance?
The second week I believed it. The fourth I
rejected it and much else loved, until the eyes
teared those last days and the lab phoned.

Back at the clinic—someone's cheap cologne,
Sunday lamb yet on the tongue, the mind cool as a pitcher
of milk, a woman's knitting needles aflutter,
Angel's hand in mind—I watched the verdict-lips move,
rubbed my arm, which, once pricked, had tingled then bruised.

The Roman Baths at Nîmes

In the hall of mirrors nobody speaks.
An ember smolders before hollowed cheeks.
Someone empties pockets, loose change and keys,
into a locker. My god, forgive me.
Some say love, disclosed, repels what it sees,
yet if I touch the darkness, it touches me.
In the steamroom, inconsolable tears
fall against us. In the whirlpool, my arms,
rowing through little green crests, help to steer
the body, riding against death. Yet what harm
is there in us? I swear to you, my friend,
crossarmed in a bright beach towel, turning round
to see my face in lamplight, that eye, ear
and tongue, good things, make something sweet of fear.

Carnations

At the pool he writes
letters in the shade.
There is little news to report.
Overhead Judas trees
shed red petals.
The air is scented
with body lotion.
Bathers with blue lips
shiver in the spring water.
Three guards with silver
crosses at their throats
are playing cards
in a shaft of light.
The prognosis is not good.
But what a sight he is!—
digging into a basket
of raspberries.
The briny bottled water
soothes his eroded mouth
as he speaks of his boyhood,
which was not so long ago,
in the corn fields of Illinois.
After strolling through
the ancient quarter,
he is out of breath,
so we sit beneath a plane tree
which is like a big stone church
in whose dark murals
I see that I will lose him.
If only I could say Go back! Go back!
As in Delacroix's
little masterpiece
where a Natchez child

is born in haste
on a bend of the Mississippi.
The young parents—
he in feathered headdress
and she but a necklace
of orange and green beads—
had been fleeing an army
when the labor pains began.
If only I could run a black comb
through the fatigued mother's
black hair and warn them,
You must go back!
But the little shallop,
awaiting their flight upriver,
stays parked in sand.
The sky, as if flesh,
grows black and blue.
Art, like life, is pitiless.
It is All Saints' Day.
Flower vendors are selling
carnations to adorn the dead.
Far off, an ambulance
wails on the horizon.

Torso

Propped up in bed, my narrow waist a pedestal,
I cannot think who or where I am, until
a couple, pausing in the corridor, embrace,
their pink mouths calling to mind the face
on the night table of my former self behind glass.
My temperatures chart a perilous graph,
alas, those who visit seldom touch me.
I am the white, embroidered glove longing to be
tugged upon a cadet's hand. "Let me die!"
I implore, but each night the village clocks, dry-eyed,
force me to live another day. Like gods,
they are jealous of one another. As if a marauding
heart is all I am, or was, and the pink dot
on the monitor a marker for the one I sought.

Paper Dolls

To some it might
have seemed vulgar
or degrading that
he was naked,
but for a wrinkled sheet.
Straight as candles,
his legs exposed
the eroding candelabrum
that was his body.
As directed,
no priest was present.
So when his mouth,
chapped and bleeding,
locked on a breath
we believed was the last,
the other of us
ran wailing down
the long blue corridor
for a nurse
who came to us
as Demeter had
to the frozen earth.
On the windowsill,
red tulips
stopped their grieving
as we kissed
what remained
good-bye
in a scene
at first holy,
then lurid,
as something stirred
beneath the sheet.

On the night table,
paper dolls cut
like shackled lions
roared at his entrance.

Supper with Roy

Still in a sweat from the thirty
odd blocks between us, I sit on the terrace
drinking vodka and lemon juice. Dirty
pigeons fly up and down to visit us,
in 16G, astonished, then worried,
to find your dread owl's yellow glass
eyes fixing on them instead. *Hurry,*
I taunt them, *Or he'll put you in his stew!*
Then through the picture window I see you:

barefooted—a hayseed on Sutton Place—
stirring a martini, in worn Levis
and your pharmacist-daddy's pink face.
A man's lot is not made easier by
what he owns, and you're a textbook case:
when you think of the day our Billy died,
even your eight sculpted Picasso plates,
their perplexed faces beholding us dine,
begin to cry: it's no subtle sign.

In between courses you smoke a Carlton.
Alfonso, your seal-point, rushes to you,
not unlike the way snow leopards did when
we once visited them at the Bronx Zoo.
If I digress on art or religion
(leaving my silver dessert spoon unused,
surest sign of my humble origins),
you smile, blowing out candles as I talk,
long-suffering as your grandmother clock.

From the living room I watch the big red
Pepsi-Cola sign glow addictively
across the East River. You stretch out dead
on the carpet, letting Alfonso knead
your chest. I sit, poet, in the loveseat,
as you recount what sultry Dietrich said
to Auden at a swank cocktail party
way back when. The steady, far-sighted gaze,
the voice from Macon: these are things I praise.

Black night has brought the message of night.
On the street a model in gold lamé
is posing in eerie white studio lights
with your handsome Greek doorman. You could say
that from Billy, whom we consigned to light
of flame, a friendship grew where ashes lay,
that he instructs, admonishes, even tonight
as we soap and rinse each porcelain dish,
sit down with wine, fruit pie and your amaryllis.

Christmas in Carthage

for Jerl Surratt and Paul Young

The great hobbler is pain, not age,
    a man writes from bed,
        the pain at the center of his body abating,
    for youth has the "better" life ahead,
      beyond the darting nurses
in the corridor where foam, hospital slippers
      and a voluminous, blue, dotted gown seemed to move
        apart from his body,
toward the padded table, an umbrella-tree of lights,
        eight silent, white figures,
    a cold hand rubbing his stomach,
his doctor's rueful smile, and then the mask.

It was the city of morphine, not Carthage,
    that rose in his mind's eye.
        The ancient North African suburb,
    where Dido, poor thing, once escaped her brother,
      was far off as the face, the only face
of a god the man longed for yet could not have,
      and so the prospect of surgery pleased him,
        knowing the gas would stop his yearning,
that the Angel of History was a grave
        in whose dark rectangle
      one heart infects another, and that it was a Christmas,
like Dido's hopeless marriage bet, that could not be.

Now all the man has is the lost face floating in his head,
    as on a pillow next to his. The silk ties
        they liked to share, yanked from their rack
    and tangled on the closet floor, have been forgotten.
    A box of dates awaits his recovery.
Four million vessels pulse with the brain's blood-sap.

The hidden stitches rot in a cluster
of vascular sharps and flats.
The Gulf of Tunis, though tainted and fished out,
remains safe anchorage in his imagination,
where there is a life, an Everyman's paradise
of open-air porticoes and fruit and love and cremation.

Little G Minor Lament

At the flea market a friend paid
a song for a watercolor
portrait of an officer he said
resembled a boy he once knew.

It was years ago at a camp,
where youths went to anneal themselves.
Like a lithograph on a stamp,
love had not relinquished itself.

In the picture, flamboyant palms
wave symbolically from a beach.
The Pacific is green as crème
de menthe, a calm sky blue as bleach.

On the destroyer's tidy deck,
instead of gin and cigarettes,
an iridescent black flyspeck,
like a man's imagination,

appears trapped behind a window.
The captain's perfect mermaid lips
are drawn like a cupid's bow,
his face is pink as a German's,

betraying, my friend speculates,
the artist's own repressed feelings.
A theory he now complicates
("ample make this bed!"), revealing

what he must have known all along:
"Lawrence," circa 1945,
begat the son whom thereupon
my friend met paddling a canoe.

But not until a mushroom cloud
rose above the painted lagoon,
and children heard queer words, heads bowed:
atom, fission, radiation.

Plastilina

It was a game of Truth more than Dare:
each of us revealing something intimate
to the others. What was there to fear,
visible only from our pink necks up?

When a pear-shaped man joined us in the tub,
I tried not to stare at the earrings
in his nipples. The filter went *glub-glub*,
swallowing the green, concentric ripples

his body made. An ugly yellow cat, lying
on the deck, lifted its head and roared
at us like the Metro-Goldwyn lion.
The thermostat checked, our testimonies resumed.

A Christian boy went first, unburdening
himself with the pleasure of a sinner
who'd brought about the undoing
of a foolish rural minister.

"Jesus brings His own rewards," he said blithely.
Oh, to be aloof as adulterous stray cats,
who gaze at us with bedroom eyes, politely
feeling nothing! Instead, memory,

"the key to everything," clings like lint
on a black velvet sofa, or a rooster's red crown
(the cock, remember, helped Peter repent),
perched insistently on its crowing head—

urging each of us, in accordance with laws
set down at the start, to recall some painful thing:
The one who'd kidnapped his son from in-laws.
The one who'd been shot at a post office.

The one who'd seen the Virgin illuminated.
The one who'd slept with a brother.
Unlike earth, which hardens, crusts, deteriorates,
the mind (or is it the heart, really?), once smothered,

recasts itself like the sculptor's dove-gray matter,
by degrees relief, medallion, small figurine:
whatever sad thing it was, mere fodder
for what, years hence, it might blissfully be.

Palm Court

A pendant glistened at your throat.
    Rain tambourined on the stately square.
White gloves and a brocaded coat
    stood watch at a threshold of frosted glass.
        We were still in our teens and emboldened
        to climb the long steps from pink into gold.

There was a cello, fluted columns
    with acanthus leaves, a checkered
marble floor, and at each table a font
    where the heart was dipped and cured.
        Green steam spiralled from our teacups.
        Face to face, we sat as on a tiered cake.

Our clothes were wet as though from weeping.
    Your hair tearing on your collar
as we ate parfaits with blue syrup
    luminous as human arteries.
        Between us, lingering like cologne, was
        a vague Dickensian sadness.

Suffering had been such a phantom thing,
    like God who we believed would shelter us,
that when sweet new consecrates of flesh
    appeared in us, fierce and unblushing,
        it seemed America was far away,
        leaving our boy-girl bodies to conform or stray.

Then a pale young moon cut across the city.
    Home was a locked up little church
that would not let us in. The century
    seemed to darken with wrath. And Earth's
        long glance into our gene pool of loving
        brought us everything and nothing.

You Come When I Call You

I was very trusting and very dangerous
the night Committee Members arrived.
Something that smelled like wet dog wrapped my eyes.
Sleeping naked, I was permitted to dress,
as someone explained how by white- and black-
ball election I was last among their choices.
At first, the friendly timbre of the voices
comforted me . . . until I was prodded like an ass
into a truck (or like the missing child Jed,
I remember thinking, whose face appeared
on my milk carton), where I could hear
others, like me, breathing prostrate on the flatbed
and the zealous talk of Brotherhood
at their seats in the cab. Drinking from flasks,
they jeered at us in our doggy masks.
Though we could not see, how we understood!

They steered us to a lake in the Commonwealth,
and, speaking in a language designated
by little Greek letters, revealed themselves
as a court for the uninitiated.
A man must make do the best he can
in a world where goodness is stamped out:
that much I resolved that humid morning South
as I drank, kneeling like a broken man,
from a sulfur spring with other Pledges,
then pressed my lips in adoration to pages
of a book held before me. "A French kiss!
She's giving it the tongue!" the Chairman hissed.
Then suddenly the proceedings ended.

My wrists and red eyes untied, I was asked
to sing songs the Little Sisters, steadfast
behind their Brothers, belted out. Legends
of Reconstruction teach us a few good things.
About pride, for instance, and how a ruined
land with hospitals and barracks was soon
our little college. Yet in that lamentable
fraternal Gamma code I found not one
natural Brother, only niggling dues to be paid,
committees, like dogs paraded
on leashes, straining towards women,
immolation of spirit, a berated
God, nobility worn like a harness,
a sour apple in the heart, and this,
this was the congenial state I'd awaited.

II

The Bird Show at Aubagne

for Nina Bohlen

The lovebirds were shouting at us when we arrived.
Then a mynah called to Nina in better French than mine,

"I am Socrates." And through miracles of genetics
he probably was. There was a society finch,

sitting on everyone's eggs, and a big Texan pigeon,
napping in the white, Provençal sun.

Potted cyclamens adorned the roofs of all the cages
wherein the pretty, aristocratic canaries, bright as sorbets,

posed like my hometown Azalea Queen who could not sing.
Mutants bred for such exquisite poise and coloring

their voices faded into recessive genes.
In another life, trained in Pavlovian teams,

they'd have launched into the smoothest, ethereal song.
If extracting art from nature belonged,

as I dream of it being, to my second nature,
bright, pointillist dots in a baby's bill would appear

on my canvas as Seurat-like lanterns for luring insects.
The Lady Goulds—named posthumously for Her Ladyship,

who painted them but let her husband steal her thunder—
wore carnal black beaks while mating with each other.

There was a silky hen, named Francoise, with a funny hat,
a Princess of Wales, from Australia, with so long a tail that

I could not help plucking myself a pastel quill,
and even a harlot with calloused feet, called a Parisian frill.

At one display six angry, Indian parakeets hung
upside-down from skinny Gandhi legs and shook their cage.

We knew what they were saying and gave them our baguettes.
Afterwards, at the Bar des Oiseaux, dusting millet

and straw from our shoes, we watched the sensible Emersonian
    ducks
glide through their little bamboo bridge towards us,

and brimming with café au lait, waved to Socrates good-bye,
to which wisdom's deep voice—"Je suis Socrate."—replied.

The Minimum Circus

for Mary Doyle Springer

From the marks on their coats
and the unambiguous wag
of their tails as they sniff
each other, one can see they are
related—all the dogs
in our neighborhood circling a quay
in the port, awaiting
the circus pushcart carrying
four dazed French housecats, who,
unperplexed, crawl through tubes, jump hoops,
balance on a highwire,
and ride bareback an irritable goat.

The sweet ringmaster, who
has no teeth, wears Cézanne's straw-hat
and borrowed evening tails.
It has taken him years to stage
the flawless "tigres" act.
He has a distant, sympathetic heart.
When Madame Pompinette,
a pretty white thing, is let out
of her little wood box,
she does ballerina stretches,
carefully licking each
murderous claw, making the dogs go wild.

Backed up on their haunches,
with pointed ears, they do not hear
moody Debussy as
Madame crosses a perilous
clothesline to her platform
and relaxes. Welcome as tears boldly

shed, the cats transcend class.
Coming no less from Arab shacks
on vineyards than from big
summer châteaux, the hounds escape
their odious lot,
drinking and drinking in the cats who eat

sardines and seem to laugh.
When the ringmaster's hat is passed,
he cracks his lion-whip
like Mallarmé yearning for some
daring, inward effect.
My ten franc piece hardly speaks to the cats,
who repose with laissez-faire
expressions like humans given
a mask, willing to tell
the truth of their predicament,
as if to say to me:
"Well, this is what life is supposed to be."

Aix

Henceforth what had lain   in the detestable square
where the pink exacto-   knife blade of the guillotine
once fell, would change me: the sun cart-wheeling
into evening; the lazy   scorpion, jeweled on the trough rim,
lifting his pincers   like a Roman athlete,
his tail erectile   and tipped with a sting,
as I splashed the slightly   radio-active fountain
on my face; the violet-man   dropping his sad bouquets;
and far off, expensive drinks   reanimating a terrace.
No more complex a thing than   one man cutting another.
Who chooses this end makes   sorrow.
Above us in her lacy niche   a dusty Virgin
ornamented the long,   patrician avenue.
Though her sculpted   gown was overgrown with ivy,
her crown shone bright   as a musical toy's.
What could she have been   pointing to from the eaves
for her child to see   but each of us —
the man of cloth hurrying   from his bell-tower,
the flesh of the fallen one   half-opened, filled with roses,
the rattle of coins from   the dark one who fled,
and me, foolish witness —   caught
in a tapestry anonymous   and faded as the human race?

Harvard Classics

It is the hour of lamps.
On our knees my mother
and I, still young, color
with crayons threadbare nap

on the livingroom rug.
Though there is no money,
no one seems to care. We
are self-possessed as bugs

waving their antennae
through cracks in the kitchen's
linoleum floor. When
Father begins to read

from the red gilt volume
in his lap, a circle
of light encapsulates
us like hearts in a womb.

Except their marriage is
already dead. I know
this though I'm only six.
So we visit Pharoahs,

a boatman on the Nile,
Crusaders eating grapes
on a beach. Life escapes
with all its sadness while

two tragic Greek poets
inhabit Father's voice.
Who'd know I'm just a boy
when he begins a stoic

moral tale concerning
a dull provincial doctor's
young French wife. If Mother,
in French, begins to sing

to herself, I know she's
had enough. Crayon stubs
litter the crumbling rug.
Our prostrate cat sneezes

at the dust in her fur.
And cries from a swallow
remind us one swallow
doesn't make a summer.

Marius, Son of Sarkis, Named for the Roman Consul, Savior from the Barbarians, Putative Husband of Mary Magdalene

is feeding his canaries on the terrace
when the Gypsies start to sing.
Dinner candles have long guttered,
and the white sun's empty sheath littered
the room with dusk.

In the distance: barking of hounds,
static from a radio broadcast,
scraping back of chairs as the world
rises from its supper to see where the music
is coming from.

A sirocco blows the yellow feathers
almost imperceptibly. In the port,
where chariots once landed, airplanes crisscross
a perfectly inked Mediterranean line.
Of those beloved,

Marius thinks, when the tambourines start to play,
only Job, his sad finch, survives, whistling
to a melon slice as if it were the moon.
It is the end of a century. Buttonquails
undo their masks.

If Marius should ask himself, roused by the night,
Have the gods forgotten me?
the Gypsies in their caravans,
like a babel of sailors, will sing him
some vain reply.

Land of Lemons

Under burnt orange ceramic roofs
sloped whimsically as in a child's drawing,
near a stone fountain where four ornamental
dolphins blew spring water into a pool
from which pigeons and shepherds alike drank,
on a street called Repentance, in a room
overlooking a convent where the weary nuns,
wearing starched wimples, watched with joy
as I blew bubbles into the passage between us,
I lived, that year, like a church mouse
to whom everything still seems possible;
and found cake crumbs everywhere I hunted.

All over town roosters crowed at me.
And coming home from the market, I was followed
(chased, some days!) by furry bumblebees
intoxicated by nodding sunflowers in my arms.
At noon when the villa shook as from a bomb,
it was only the housekeeper's pilot-lover
breaking the sound barrier again. Boom! Boom!
her lover went signalling her each day.
One morning under a colonnade of plane trees,
where I would go for coffee, I met a soprano.
A little pyramid of sugar cubes rose before her
as she spoke. Deafening scooters dashed by.

Inside the café, the mournful shriek of steam
through shiny espresso machines seemed in keeping
since it was Lent, though what we believed was uncertain.
Much later I would learn of the electrician,
who raised ducks and kissed her hands in the old
provincial fashion after they'd made love.
It was he she pondered, though the affair had ended

and he was not yet dead, when two Moroccans
in bright turbans unrolled a carpet before us
and perched on it with the loose sleeves
of their djellabahs reversed, freeing their arms.
One with bracelets and a Timex watch played a horn.

The other, with painted nails, uncoiled
from a hatbox two cobras, with inflated
neck hoods, which brushed against and imitated
one another in an amusingly lurid fashion.
It was not until long afterward that she revealed
to me how the charmed serpents that afternoon
had signified what irreparable harm
had already been done to her by her lover's
smoldering daisy chain of virus.
As we contemplated it, even the ethereal
freesia seemed to fall into decline.
When our hopes turned the color of grey pearl,

lovely pigments of green which once shaded us
from the bleaching sun turned pale as flesh
preserved in formaldehyde. When each day
began to menace us like a bloody mattress,
we set off into a fairy tale of brother and sister
equally facing the unknowable night.
On a narrow dog's trail, in a secluded valley
with a hermit's farm, we drank greedily from The Source
alongside the hermit's cattle; below a ruined city
perched on a crest, we slept, like death itself,
though a nightingale's indelicate call each night
trailed repeatedly from a cypress hedge;

under a triumphal arch garlanded with chained
prisoners, fruits and flowers, we hid unafraid
as soldiers on reconnaissance disappeared
in the fog; in a salt marsh favored by Gypsies,

we rode robust white ponies and melancholy bulls.
Even when a mistral heightened claims made on us
by ordinary life and the dark blue sea snapped
like a wet loose sail, we stumbled on a place
in a field of waving rape where gigantic
steel pylons, shouldering high-voltage wires,
stood erect as stick-figure men drawn to defend
us and the wild unaffected poppies.

The Housekeeper and the Handyman

The old port's modern armada
is setting sail. Restless Mediterranean
waves rise metrically and break
against its tall spears. A wet lighthouse
trembles on the jetty, its plainspoken
beacon a steady, broken sentence.

The dream-ships are a lucky sentence
for the boys borne away on the armada.
Their girls, in fishnet-stockings, cannot speak
or believe it, their Mediterranean
blue eye makeup smeared on their cheeks. What's a house
without a man's exacting love at breakfast?

That's what they're thinking, their earrings breaking
against their necks like anchors, the sentence
draining them like the moan of the lighthouse.
Could it be so much sadness becomes the armada,
straining for the deep Mediterranean?
Even the black rocks are tear-streaked and speechless.

If only the old villa could speak,
beneath whose mansard roof a couple breaks
from their warm sheets. "The Mediterranean
is a Rorschach test," it would say. Sentences
it makes us phrase, as with the armada,
tell us who we are: The couple in the empty house

are more than "the help," the housekeeper
having found self-knowledge in a—plainly speaking—
loveless affair. The armada
is spouting vapor like the breakfast
teakettle in the villa. Vague sentences
reveal a morning after, until the Mediterranean

concocts, as the Mediterranean
does, another flamboyant day. The lighthouse
is a white spire of sugar cubes. A sentence
is played on the harpsichord that has not spoken
all winter, the handyman's hands breaking
the silence. Fishing smacks replace the armada.

The housekeeper puts her hair in a net, her broken,
Mediterranean bobby pins, in perfect X's, speaking
a coded sentence of survival to the armada.

Three Aurelian Moons

CASSIS

It was a mackerel sky that engulfed them,
three skin divers hunting our stretch of beach.
And if you listened carefully, bleaching
out the sea, there was a cuckoo clock's ten
mechanical cries, then the pealing out
of a congregation's glad Wesley hymn.
On the jetty a litter of kittens
tugged madly at their supper of red mullet.
It was Assumption Day and Mary blew
into the fishermen's sails. When the spruce green
tungsten of the lighthouse pulsed, if you
squinted, a shelf of reddish cliffs, like a horned beak,
seemed to rise from the sea. They say the view
is so pretty there, it's the suicide's favorite leap.

MONT SAINTE-VICTOIRE

To village children sleeping in the basin,
the summit was a perfect chocolate mousse peak.
To infantry it was a sumptuous drapery,
raked by metal balls, to lose oneself within.
To migrating bats a ridge to circumvent
or live by. The white rock shone like a basket
of eggs, then disappeared like cigarette ash.
Secretly the mountain, tear-stained, meant
for us to recognize a lesson in regrets: Landscape,
it was saying, like art, is only a pleasant trope;
a baby's room, even grim, is sweeter than muscat grapes,
for each birth stirs in us rivulets of hope.
And the plane trees agreed, showing us their waists,
where soldiers carved hearts with the heart's knife strokes.

LES BAUX

As in some parody of fallen nations,
Zelda, our cocker spaniel, was blown away from us,
like a handkerchief, and set down by an anxious
mistral near the crumbling limestone mansions.
Pale as Spanish tobacco, our rented Peugeot
had crept along the route of Christmas processions—
Kelli and Rex lost in darkening digressions—
toward the perilous, wind-buffeted plateau.
Zelda's sigh alone rose above war's ruin.
Combing the rock with a strangely human frown,
could she sense our disbelief—a *fin de siècle* moon
painting our brows? Bent to the wind even now
in that memory, I see a hare, rusting plumes
of maize and how a life, mine, once stopped, moved anyhow.

Palette

Lying on the floor of Anna's studio,
I view her from the same angle as Nick,
her Boston terrier. The upright piano's
been playing jazz. We're all a little homesick.

Anna's hair is silky red and the hairs
of her paintbrush Prussian blue. There's a landscape
on her easel. Bonnard is in her head. If I dare
speak of rent or Nick's incurable gas, she rubs her nape,

glances at me, then goes on painting.
Tulips in the carafe are chrome yellow.
Parasol pines in the garden are faintly
disorienting, as if innocent Rousseau

had made them from broccoli stalks.
When Anna squeezes a tube of cinnabar green,
her face twists like Madame Cézanne's. And Nick?—
stirring as if he spots the resemblance—from between

my legs gives a pug's "how 'bout that" grunt.
A mistral is riffling Anna's unanswered letters.
The sky is burnt lake, auguring blood in the months
ahead, they say . . . until Anna rubs it out forever.

Irradiation

The evening began like any other:
the sky shone phosphorus,
marbling the villa's granite terrace.
First-born, Madeleine, bounced on my lap.
Foolish Henna chased around her poodle self.
Wine splashed to the goblet's rim.
Idle talk of lemons at the market,
the weeping icon stolen from our local parish.
Some heartless joke from our patriarch.
Then grunting and gnashing in a shelf
of pines above. Something near human,
yet animal, moaned. Henna pressed at our heels.
"They've got the neighbor's pup," June cried.
Bristling, on cloven hooves, wild boars dragged it away.
"Mother Nature strikes again," someone said,
Father Time the truer agent.
Gerard took a mean drag on his Gauloise,
excused himself to carry Madeleine to bed.
The grim scene smoldered in each of us,
the heart excavating itself:

        All I could see
was you napping in the backseat at The Cedar Forest,
an ethereal place dating from Gaul,
dozens of thick, brindled snouts
and stiff, corkscrew tails trotting
through the campsite as if to reclaim it,
then bowling along your Citroën's fenders.
Here the mind censors itself: You are stumbling
towards me after the incident,
your green cotton shift stained,
leg and arm scratches pink as brain tissue
on the glass slide where abstracted thought

meets violent vision. Your eyes, distracted, fix on mine.
A string of cultured pearls breaks
against your collarbone. Your lips are murder red,
like Madeleine's cooing in her crib.

Eating Figs under the White Rocks

You were saying something about your father,
whose hair you'd shampooed that morning.

The dogs were gamboling on the lawn.
Three pines stood immense, like your brothers, before us.

Honeybees, vaguely eupeptic, made arabesques in the lavender.
Clippings from your father's nails littered the patio.

A figure moved through the emerald pool,
swimming as across a Japanese screen.

The planted pots of Love-lies-bleeding
spoke only of loss to the blue hummingbird that wanted them.

Telephone wires made a score in the sky
the terrible grackles could not sing.

Pink powder balls on the mimosa tossed in the wind,
pretending to dust a dowager's cheeks.

Head and body withdrawn, or almost, a mollusk
inscribed something neither you nor I could read

on a giant sunflower's leaf,
unless, that is, it only said what we'd always known:

that unlike the chorus of molting cicadas
transmitting on wavelengths far off as Eden,

none of us—not your father napping in a slingchair
or even you, who would betray me—could ever return again.

Une Lettre à New York

If it's spring in the city, have the marchers,
each one with a shrieking whistle, short-circuited the streets,
their cause as grave as the dirty cabs growling at their feet?
Is Paul Taylor at the City Center? Has my architecture-
grad-student-subtenant remembered Sting, a pet squirrel
whose appearance each May on the fire escape ledge
is as celebrated as our pink dogwood's flowering? Privileged
as she is, eating Arabian almonds all these years, if she's early
and hears me in the shower, she knows to come right in.
Will Joe, my Italian barber, still tell me what to do in life,
reading my moods in his mirror—his razor like a fruit knife
against the peach's flesh instead of the proud artist's chin?
Will a burglar have borrowed my red Schwinn from the rooftop,
the rusty chain foiling a smooth delirious escape?
With pompoms swinging on their skimmers like grapes,
does a Colombian troupe still serenade commuters stopped,
even in gray business suits, by a tug on the heartstrings,
the subway chasm converted into a dream of disembarking?
Does the beggar on my block, who says his name is Marx,
still wear a deeper tan than mine? Will souls of three sleeping
friends—May, Lola and Vladimir—visit in the evening,
arranging themselves in the ailanthus outside my window?
If they smile and blink as from some Broadway video,
it will be an urban bequest for those who could not say good-bye,
their numinous bodies dissolving then into July's fireflies,
whose lanterns alchemize my cheap paper shades into Chinese
    silk.
Each of you who writes reports illness, pain from love spilt,
or someone who's gone to the other side, yet correspondence tries
to be uplifting, disproving Judas who writes man's sad history.
Could he have been right who said there was earth and man
in the beginning, that we created God, that we created Heaven,
in our want or need for something more than awful elegy?

The little island wedged between three rivers,
from which our letters come and go, is the personification of
   hope.
The buildings are black and white like sonnets. And enveloped
in between, the first sweet cherries of the season are being
   delivered.

III

Crayola

Pixilated
beneath a cloud-
burst of shower spray,
a swimteam trio
of butterfly pros,

little mermen
in the gym's
surfeit of Adams,
still goggled and brimmed
with victory, soaked

through as tadpoles—
a duo birthday-
suited and "J"
sporting a scarlet Speedo
bright as a matador

cape—cavort
their trinity of
umbilical love
through an opaline
zeppelin of steam,

rippling like cartoon
boys begot in foam,
as I tiptoe
across blue tiles, shampoo
stinging my eyes.

Swimming with the Dead

Pink chemicals in the school pool—not you,
in whites, saying *This is what I've chosen,*
your meaning subtle as a dagger tattoo—

make a teary mess of me. Oceans
of nerve gas, not camels or Arabian sand,
mark the life we both know you have chosen.

In the Red Sea a frigate of sheep is stranded,
far, far from Mother's yellow breakfast table,
where, apart from nerve gas, camels and you tanned,

she sees a desert in her sugar bowl.
If only a rescue froggy hovered overhead!
Far, far from Mother's yellow breakfast table,

my school pool is like a war grid. The Grateful Dead
are on the radio, their electric guitars
grinding like a froggy dangled overhead.

If I hold my breath as long as I can, there are
goatherds tending their flocks, bomblets of shooting stars,
and, born out of pink chemicals, you
in a poncho showing off a dagger tattoo.

WINTER *1991*

54

Tarantula

At a petshop in the village,
in a battered gothic cage,
he stood guard (or was kept hostage?)

at a little parapet trap-
door. His dirty home was so sad,
his burrow a curled up scrap

of carpet, that I unscrewed
the wire gate with my Swiss knife—DO
NOT UNSCREW! it read—and let him through.

Ten stiff bristles uplifted him,
each a comb for his hairy abdomen,
his front legs now and again

waving in an attitude of bliss
as he swayed upon my wrist.
Then gliding like a dugout canoe, its

oars moving in a phalanx,
he rowed across my long arm, strangely
beautiful as the human brain

shining through profligate grief.
When he looked at me with a queer
air, nearsighted as I, did he make me

out to be a giant fern, his perch,
as I have made him now into a verse?
When his creaky spinneret stirred,

I felt guilt—watching him create
a silky floating line in haste—
knowing a sad house has no escape.

The Cabbage Butterfly

Something like volcanic ash wafted in air.
Then drizzle, as if the saints were pissing on us.
A beggar's accordion. Dribbling chin-sweat.
"Up there's where Kong climbed with that pretty blonde,"
a perfumed brunette was telling her son,
whose red face made no response
as she pointed through subway gratings above.
Tenacious as a black beetle spawned
from some hot, perfidious underworld,
ours was a dim, sultry place
with crow-like markings on the walls,
where a man in uniform sat beside me,
his tired, handsome face marked by wens.
All of us feeling bombsite black,
metal portals opened to a bulldog-shove,
pounding like blood through valves of my heart,
when overhead, flapping against a backdraft,
a creamy cabbage butterfly arrived.
Attaching itself like a drift of silk
to my brow, it was lighter than a dollar,
yet nourished me like manna where I stood.

Wedding Announcement

Appearing in the *Times*
Sunday, a simple tale
of love less than sublime,
though born of class at Yale.

The bride, of (as they say)
Locust Valley, wore your
basic Scaasi. Nosegays
of crocus shone light for

Mummy's pearls at her ears.
Daddy, Chairman at Dupont,
gave her away with fears
still for his debutante:

a groom from Kentucky,
whose breed of thoroughbred,
alas, had no derby.
Real estate—one read

between lines of cold type—
was keeping him solvent.
Anyhow, who could gripe
about ill-involvements

in a Rockefeller?
Not the Right Reverend
at St. Bart's, whose larder
was stocked with Cornish hens,

port and Stilton cheese.
At the ceremony,
a poem was read that pleased
most assembled: Money,

it seemed to say, was nothing
next to mercy, humor,
a quest for truth. Giving
their assent with fervor,

congregants rose, straightened
their spines, beholding
the bride, who'd squared, by then,
her lovely tanned shoulders,

as a princess
might have on her pony,
long before one sprayed locusts
in Locust Valley.

Katrina's Bedroom

Absolute attention is prayer. SIMONE WEIL

Waterpots of the sky
in ready-to-pour condition,
a rumbling wakens me —
bewilderment of self
fallen away —
on a big brass bed
facing hemlocks.

A startled monarch,
caught on the window ledge
in a metallic grackle's beak,
flapping, flapping
like a mechanical toy,
makes me think of something
a friend once said:

"Ignorant life always
disrupts the nostalgic plots
of scripture." Then
a wind, released
like a deep,
deep drag on a cigarette,
blows them both away.

Something that sounds
like hooves of geldings
in a neighbor's paddock
clip clop
across the copper rooftop.
White, white wicker chairs
look at one another, empty,

empty as a page
on the desk looking at me,
that looked at Howard and May
and Sylvia before me.
Pacing the oriental rug,
splashing in the princely tub,
reading Baudelaire

on the flowered settee,
I see them opening and closing
my eighteen windows
whose crosshatched leaded glass
is framed as if by the mind's
prosodic lattice,
teaching the poet to climb and climb.

Against the picture window,
my battered lunch pail
looks like a little red barn,
its red thermos a fodder silo.
Rain eddies on the glass
as in a wash basin,
or movie of a cyclone.

When the power flicks off
and a baby fox scurries
across the lawn,
shoving its snout
in its mother's groin,
ignorant thought in the mansion,
undisturbed, burns on and on.

The Christological Year

on my birthday

The record skips in the parlor
as the gurney wheels pass.
Mother's on her way to maternity.
On the 16th green Father's putt misses its cup,
his Japanese caddie tuning the instrument
of his mind Buddha-fashion in the grass.
A cosmographer's blue Pacific sea
illuminates the horizon.
West is far away as sentimental honeymoon years
wavering in a crater of Nevada sunlight.
I am nowhere and everywhere.
A vague shape in a blue peignoir
(could it have been a kimono?)
holds me in its arms.

A sleep-inducing sickness takes me from myself.
Dust on the shelf where figures once stood
maps a world that will meet in me:
Father's walkie-talkie voice from the Arctic;
the Venus-fly-trap locking its teeth
on Mother's diamond ring;
wigwams pitched in the Shenandoah;
my saucy angelfish, who ate his wife,
and my old world chameleon,
whose stomach for houseflies was prodigious;
a six-ton black-and-white orca, midair,
his flippers grasped by a trainer
straddling him bareback;
the child's psychopathology
of lying to keep adulthood at bay;
the Caspian and Black Seas sweeping Noah and me away;
three days of hiccoughing nervously;
The Visible Man's motor and visceral nerves,

a fulcrum of red and blue;
body rashes; blood chemistries;
astigmatic visions of ecstasy in a tidewater bog;
offertory baskets carrying our quarters away
(would He take me too?); Miss Mellow —
I cut her lawn — who secretly was a man;
bolstering a brooding, besotted parent;
a playmate's cleft palate,
the hairline fissure holding me in thrall;
the branch of rainless lightning that took Scotty,
leviathans thrashing us, at Hatteras;
the forbidden wish — to be dead — granted;
a railcar bearing you towards me.

My thirty-third summer.
The dispassionate lake of adulthood widening.
At the playground a fountain
still bubbles on the lawn.
Could I ever not reach the jet to slake my thirst?
In our classroom, on the science wall,
at the round earth's imagined corners,
cherubim rehearse their trumpets.
We are in the ultra-violet past:
I am partly in an everglade,
partly on an iceberg.
Just as now, while a bee drones about my wrist,
the lilacs on my desk droop their heavy heads,
letting fall a kind of purple, metaphysical spray.

The House Guest Looks at Love and Life

At other people's houses, at motels
and at home, he makes his bed before breakfast
with hospital corners folded as neatly
as the collar of a man's shirt. A perfect guest,
his presence is felt by his gift for what
friends regard as his charming invisibility . . .
a perfect guest to all, that is, except
the household's affection-hungry kitty,
who knows a man by his lap, and demands
it be surrendered. Even standing bare, whichever
way he turns he leaves no traces: the bed
that looks unslept-in; the bathroom mirror
rubbed of fog; the bright shower stall rinsed
of wiry gray hairs weeded from his chest.
And most of the time he is happy since
no one guesses what was so cleverly repressed:

a swine's fear of knives or anything sharp
or pointed; hearing things so well it
troubles him; a redneck's hardness of heart
(thanks to his father); a dread, an infinite
foreboding before the sea. Of course, there's more:
how he wears himself down understanding too much;
how he believes Christ made wine out of water;
how he has difficulty starting his urine. Touch
him unexpectedly, though, and the doors
of his face open like foliage or wings
on a dragonfly. Without even blushing,
the face that was frozen becomes a Labrador's.
All he ever wanted, you see, was not
so much a place but himself whole again,
before his conscience, like a glowworm caught
in a jar, shone its gaudy light through him.

Buddha and the Seven Tiger Cubs

Holding a varnished paper parasol,
the gardener—a shy man-off-the-street—
ripple-rakes the white sand, despite rainfall,
into a pattern effortlessly neat,
meant to suggest, only abstractly, the sea,
as eight weathered stones are meant to depict
Buddha and the hungry cubs he knows he
must sacrifice himself to feed. I sit
in a little red gazebo and think —
as the Zen monks do — about what love means,
unashamed to have known it as something
tawdry and elusive from watching lean
erotic dancers in one of the dives
on Stark Street, where I go some lovesick nights.

Even in costume they look underage,
despite hard physiques and frozen glances
perfected for the ugly, floodlit stage,
where they are stranded like fish. What enhances
their act is that we're an obedient crowd,
rheumy with liquor; our stinginess
is broken. When one slings his leg proudly
across the bar rail where I sit, I kiss
a five dollar bill and tuck it in his belt.
He's a black swan straining its elastic
neck to eat bread crumbs and nourish itself.
My heart is not alert; I am transfixed,
loving him as tiger cubs love their
mother who abandons them forever.

Apostasy

Father, when, when, when will you lift me,
dirty baby, from my crib?
With pail and shovel, I dig, dig for you,
scratching the earth like a hen.
When I pull her chord, my mermaid doll,
with flaxen hair, says strange things —
"Sooner dead than changed!"
Could she be speaking of you, Father?
Well, if that's what Mermaid believes,
Mermaid cannot come to tea.
Or the others, Father, piled like puppies
at my feet: nursing shark, green toad
with red tongue, rubber goldfish —
who come to parties I set for them
with Mother's blue Fiestaware,
singing Hawaiian songs, eating shortbread.
"Dirty Baby, Dirty Baby," you say to me
when I nuzzle my wet face against your neck.
Dirty Baby loves the taste of flesh.
Dirty Baby needs you to cut his meat.
Dirty Baby needs you to teach him how to chew.

Ex-voto

At the garden party all talk
is of conversions. Our hostess,
a nervous woman, confesses
a weakness for religious art
where human grief is averted
owing to the Virgin, as in
an icon painted in 1910
hanging in her den. Wearing blue skirts
bloated like parachutes, two small
sisters are dragged from the sea
beneath the village wharf. Could it be
their wooden shoes that made them fall?

In an Oz-like skyscape,
wearing a gold and velvet crown,
Mary lifts her arms above the town
from beneath a white ermine cape.
On their knees, the little girls
use their first miraculous breaths
to pray in gratitude. When pressed
to remember herself in their world,
our friend reveals how as a girl,
of fourteen maybe, she ran away,
living as a sort of protégée
to a man who kept her.

Together they did heroin,
had a child. After a few years
she phoned her parents, who volunteered
to come and get her. "Loving him
was easy," she allows, eyes downcast,
"while I believed I was wounded."
Life since has been strewn

with failed retellings of the past.
On the lawn she wears sandals
like Jesus. A little cross
at her neck accents what was lost.
Then another of us rambles:

"Hey, in the South of France, I toured
the grotto of Mary Magdalene."
Thrown in a boat for martyrdom,
without sails, rudders, or oars,
she foresaw a certain, horrible death.
Yet the sacred barque floated in calm.
Having known the flesh, she practiced lifelong
penitence, dwelling in a forest.
In the mountain cave where she slept,
a somber place dripping with dew,
one radiant sunflower grew.
"At the sight of it many wept."

Couldn't it be too much is made
of our conversions, when in fact
they happen — though not dramatic
or miraculous — in small ways
every day? As I am converted
from boredom to elation
when a swarm of bees hastens
upon our gathering; though squirted
with gas, they seem too cheerfully
engorged with honey to sting and ascend
peaceably into the air, like women
taking baskets home, unadmittedly heavy.

Immaculate Mary
Breathes the Air We Breathe

Immaculate Mary breathed the air we breathed
and felt no pain as she arrived today
borne on the shoulders of four solemn ushers,
who wore wrinkled suits and looked as if they believed
she'd come, indeed, from Albany to say
a word or two to those who'd doubted her.
"I've just met the prettiest girl,"
the wifeless deacon said, "in the whole world!" —

though it was only a framed replica
of the pregnant Mother of God as she
appeared to Juan Diego on his cactus-
fiber cloak — now at a basilica
near Mexico City — her effigy
converting nine million Aztecs to Catholics.
You'd think its apostolic work was done,
or at least curtailed since 1531.

On the church lawn a mower chewed a hank
of weeds as we, the faithful, sat or knelt —
some with our buttocks girdered by a pew —
impassively. The acrid air stank
with the odor of cut grass. What I felt
was like a dizziness from the flu,
then redness more anger than fever:
afflictions of any unbeliever.

Had Our Lady of Guadalupe, whose name
was thought to mean "river of light,"
really come so far to end abortion —
she who gave her son in sacrifice claim
now some suit against us? On a powder-white
petition card I wrote, without caution,

something cold a realist might say, let it
be burned like a love letter in a basket,

remembering a friend, now dead, who indulged
me once with a gift of water brought from Lourdes
in a green bottle shaped like the Virgin,
how when I screwed off her crown like a light bulb
and thirstily gulped, gulped the sugared
spoonfuls — suggesting amniotic currents —
I looked at my open palms hopefully,
even though I knew nothing could change me.

And He Kissed Me with the Kisses from His Mouth

In the yellow cottage
where Hansel and Gretel
might have lived,
a great solitude ended.
Gasping, half-fainting,
it departed beneath
the lintel of a green door.
Like a smooth pond,
the braided rug
encircled me, where I lay,
grasping nothing, repulsing nothing.
Then on the forest path
a bicyclist appeared,
wearing a harlequin cap,
his pedals like rhymes
carrying him towards me,
his front wheel
spraying needles of red mud
across his chest. When a flame
gutted a crackling log
on the cottage hearth,
I understood
the opposition
of birch and fire
to be true friendship,
as when he, at the pond's edge,
with a wolf's air,
undressed greedily
before me.

The New Life

Through clouds of tiny rocks
and rippling showers,
a mallard doffs
his brilliant copper-green shawl.
Sitting and watching above,
our scarlet tanager
is sick, so sick
he's missed his trip
down the Amazon.
The world is gray,
a stranger might think,
but for the freckled blue crab,
armor regal with moss,
towing sidewise,
through the rippling surface,
a cargo of eggs,
tumbling like each of us,
slave of hope,
into the purple mirror
where it is dark at first.
Can you see? A gemmed stillness.
Then copper sunlight
rains down
a heartspring of pennies.
A pyramid rises
in the hourglass again.
Our English sparrows
are half-drunk with love.
And the three-pointed leaves,
sugar-fueled and scarlet,
are waving their flame-hands
in air.

A NOTE ABOUT THE AUTHOR

Henri Cole was born in Fukuoka, Japan, in 1956. He was reared in Virginia and graduated from the College of William and Mary. He holds graduate degrees from the University of Wisconsin and Columbia University and is the recipient of fellowships from the Ingram Merrill Foundation and the National Endowment for the Arts. In 1989 he received the Amy Lowell Poetry Travelling Scholarship. His poems have been published in *Antaeus, The Atlantic, The Nation, The New Republic, The New Yorker, The Paris Review* and *The Yale Review*, among others, and he has published two previous collections of poetry: *The Marble Queen* (1986) and *The Zoo Wheel of Knowledge* (1989). From 1982 to 1988 he was executive director of the Academy of American Poets, and he has since taught at Columbia, Reed, Yale and the University of Maryland. At present he is Briggs-Copeland Lecturer in Poetry at Harvard.

A NOTE ON THE TYPE

The text of this book has been set on the Linotype in a typeface called Baskerville. It is a facsimile reproduction of types cast from molds made for John Baskerville (1706–1775) from his designs. The punches for the revived Linotype Baskerville were cut under the supervision of the English printer George W. Jones. John Baskerville's original face was one of the forerunners of the type-style known as "modern face" to printers: a "modern" of the period A.D. 1800.

Composition by
Heritage Printers, Inc., Charlotte, North Carolina.
Printed and bound by
Quebecor Printing, Kingsport, Tennessee.
Designed by Harry Ford.